MW01591196

The Journal To Joy

Dream Big!

The Journal To Joy

Weekly Reflections to Help You Experience
More Self-Love, Faith, and Happiness

JOY FITZGERALD

Mynd Matters Publishing
201 17th Street NW, Suite 300, Atlanta, GA 30363
www.myndmatterspublishing.com

ISBN-13: 978-1-948145-16-9

FIRST EDITION

In memory of my beautiful sister and angel, Shaun Skinner. You were my best friend and my source of quiet strength.

To:

____

From:

____

One of the best gifts a person can receive is a tool to help find great joy in this journey we call life. I pray this book is that tool for you!

IF YOUR GOALS DON'T SCARE YOU, THEY AREN'T BOLD ENOUGH.

THE JOURNAL TO JOY

In life, each of us is on a journey to find and maintain joy. Whether it is joy in our careers, family, faith, finances, health, or relationships, we long for fulfillment and happiness that at times might feel difficult to attain. The concept of joy in and of itself is relative as there is not a singular definition of how one experiences or defines joy—it is personal. It is based on one's inner ability to be content and ultimately, happy. In essence, it is a feeling and a state of mind of how one experiences the world and chooses to approach life.

Obtaining joy is a journey. It is a lifelong process on a winding pathway with many twists, turns, and unknowns. In the quest to be happy or find joy, it starts with understanding who you are, what has shaped your life, why you exist, what is your purpose, and how you define *your* journey. The first step is self-discovery. You must spend time and deep thought in understanding yourself in a way that creates more clarity and real vulnerability.

I unequivocally believe joy is attainable for everyone. I believe you have a purpose and divine assignment in this journey we call life. The big question is, "Are you happy?" If your answer is yes, then this journal will help heighten your happiness and propel it to new and more fulfilling levels. If your answer is no, get ready to experience a soul awakening transformation as you *journal to joy*!

The Journal to Joy is designed to provide you with weekly opportunities to engage in deep reflection and purposeful thought. It will require you to focus on yourself, your life, and areas of importance and priority. At times, it will feel somewhat scary or maybe even uncomfortable. That is okay. Just know that you are experiencing those emotions because you are learning a new mental habit and exercising a new muscle in your brain and in your heart.

The Journal to Joy can be used as a standalone opportunity of self-reflection, discovery, and goal development. It can also be used as a supplement to the book *The Journey to Joy: 5 Generations Share Stories That Every Woman Needs to Hear*. Whatever your reason, you have a divine purpose in exploring the words between the following pages. This journal provides weekly questions for reflection and affirmations to help guide you to a journey of less stress, sadness, self-doubt and unhappiness.

As I created and designed this journal, I prayed for each and every reader. I silently imagined an awakening and movement in your heart and mind that will release new joy into your life. I stand in affirmation with you so that your dreams will become new realities. It is my hope, wish, and prayer that you will obtain more love, faith, peace and joy. I am already encouraged and inspired by your purchase of ***The Journal to Joy*** as it speaks to your desire for a better life and a brighter future.

Throughout my life, reflecting has been one of the most soul healing methods I have used to help me experience joy. It has helped me to become real about who I am and acknowledge my failures, disappointments, fears, but also my accomplishments, triumphs and successes. I learned that the more I reflected, the better I became at it and so will you.

So, what do you need to do? Great question. Follow the simple steps below to maximize the benefits of this journal.

1. **Determine the best day for you to engage in reflecting.** Choose a day of the week that is the least dedicated to multiple priorities and responsibilities. For example, don't choose a day in which you have additional commitments such as choir rehearsal, dance practice, tennis, golf lessons, etc. Commit to a day and stick to it!

   What day do you commit to?_________________

2. **Select a time when you are least-likely to be interrupted.** If you have small children or there are many people in your home, it might be best to choose a time when others are asleep. This might

mean waking up thirty minutes earlier one morning a week to journal. For me, I have found it best to wait until everyone is asleep at night and then I can have my "me time."

Now this is where many people lose hope as they begin to make excuses for not having the time to reflect. Don't allow excuses to be the barrier for realizing your dreams!

What is the best time for reflection?__________

3. **Find a place that is quiet and in which you feel comfortable.** It is important to be in a location that provides safety, comfort, and privacy. Think of places such as an office, a quiet room, your favorite couch or chair, or even the restroom.

   What is a quiet place in which you find comfort?_______________________________

4. **If possible, light a candle or add an aroma that enhances the atmosphere.** Research has shown that smells and aromas influence and impact one's mood.

5. **Open your book and read the weekly quote and questions. Then, for the next seven minutes, simply reflect and write.** Be sure to set a timer on your phone. Deep reflection takes practice as we have hardwired our brains to always

be busy and avoid the "white space." For many, you will find seven minutes of reflection and writing to be somewhat challenging at first. Don't give up. Before long, you will have it mastered.

Based on my personal and professional experience, there is something magical about seven minutes. Most people can reflect for two to five minutes and then they are ready to talk or check their phones. It is difficult to focus and write for seven whole minutes. However, I have found that somewhere between five and seven minutes, people begin to go deeper and offer more vulnerably. Write whatever comes to your heart or your mind and allow yourself to be honest, even if it is scary.

6. **Inhale deeply then read what you wrote.** After you finish reading, write some more. Include additional statements or even questions. You do not have to have all of the answers and that is okay. What you express may reveal areas where you have questions and need to take more time to process and identify the answers.

   How did that feel? ________________________

   ____

7. **Write your affirmation statement.** At the end of the chapter, write one or two statements to affirm

a *new* step towards progress in your journey. A wise person once told me, "One tiny step forward is still progress."

Here are a couple of affirmation examples to give you a sense of how to affirm and speak new joy into your life:

a. I am strong, resilient, and able to overcome my fears.
b. I deserve happiness and joy.
c. I will not allow my circumstances to make me depressed.
d. I will be authentic in how others experience me today without fear of what they might think.
e. I will use my voice because it is worth hearing.
f. I am enough!

Your life is a journey and it deserves the dedicated time and attention to make it everything you ever desired, hoped, or wished for. This journey only requires one big commitment. You must commit to fifteen minutes once a week. It sounds like a lot but take a deep breath and remember, it is not that hard. If you are serious about living a more purposeful life, the big commitment should be easy. It all comes down to one critical question, "Is your happiness/joy worth a minimum of fifteen minutes once a week?" I know it is. So, let's get started!

DREAM BUILDING

One year from today, how do you want your life to look? What goals do you want to have accomplished? What new beginnings and memories do you want to create? What bad habits do you want to have stopped? These are the type of questions you should begin to ask yourself. Before we start the fifty-two weeks of reflection, let's first acknowledge and identify five goals you want to attain over the next year.

Many people become discouraged as they set big, bold, lofty goals with very little understanding of how to accomplish them. This leads to frustration and in many cases, failure. To set you up for success, let's identify goals that are realistic, inspirational and attainable.

First, choose the top areas of your life in which you want to experience joy or fulfillment. This could be your career, finances, health, family, marriage, education, relationships, parental status, mental well-being, etc. Next, think of the outcomes that you would like to achieve in those areas. For example, if you choose mental well-being as your area, one outcome could be experiencing a major holiday without being depressed. Or going one week without crying or experiencing depression. Make your goals very specific. You should be able to easily identify if the goal was accomplished or not.

Take your goals seriously and commit to them. Take one week to think long and hard about your goals. If five is too many, choose three but whatever you do, choose your goals carefully. Make a conscious effort to ensure that of the five, three of them are things you can actually accomplish. Reserve the last two goals for things that stretch you and require significant additional effort. Stretch goals should challenge you and make you somewhat uncomfortable because they will require growth and self-discovery.

Last December, my children asked a powerful and yet provocative question, "Mom, what's holding you back from accomplishing your goal of writing a book?" Admittedly, my children are a weak spot for me. My joy as a mother is the one role at which I never want to fail. It is a sacred gift to have the honor of being called a mother. I treasure their opinions of me more than I do others. So, when they asked the question, it awakened something deep in my soul. It startled me because I didn't have a *safe* answer. Deep down, I knew the real answer. I was afraid and made excuses.

Writing a book was a stretch goal that I had put on my goal list for five years but never accomplished. It was the very thing that I wanted to do but was afraid. I was afraid of what people might think if I shared personal stories. I dreaded the thought of learning the publishing process. I cringed at the idea of knowing where to begin. I questioned if my writing was good enough. I didn't think I could find the time to dedicate to such a time-intensive task such as writing. Basically, I delayed the goal every year because I was afraid.

As we sat in the family room with Christmas carols playing, fireplace lit, and Christmas décor adding a special feel and ambiance, they looked at me waiting for the answer. Then suddenly, my husband came to my rescue, or so I thought.

"Babe, what is getting in the way of you having time to write this book that I can take off your plate? Whatever it is, give it to me and I will own it. I want to do whatever I can to provide you the support and love to accomplish this dream. So now, you have no excuses!"

Wow! I was overwhelmed with emotions of love and gratefulness but also embarrassment. I was embarrassed because I felt as though I had let them all down.

That's it. I looked around the room with a spirit of courage and commitment and said, "This will be the year that I write the book." As those words began to escape my mouth, I was confessing both my fears and strong dedication to pouring my heart into this dream. Throughout the years, my mother has instilled in me, "Confession is good for the soul." Well, I guess she was right! Declaring it out loud to my family felt different and made the goal real for me. I remember the first time I said it out loud, something in the pit of my stomach awakened and it was scary. So, I began to say it over and over again, until that feeling began to dissipate.

I have always considered myself a person of my word. So, I began to tell everyone that I was writing a book this year. I told my family, friends, personal board of directors, mentors, and yes, even my boss. I needed accountability. I knew that by telling everyone, I was in fact making my dream a reality. I was making an affirmation for my future.

Commitment is more than a word. It is mental first. It starts with you. It is conceived in the mind and the spirit long before it can ever manifest itself in reality. I needed to confess as often and frequent as possible so that my mind and spirit came into agreement. When I connected both my heart and mind to the vision, then and only then did I have the power to move to action.

I now look back and laugh because those fears are hardly recognizable. Not only did I write the book, I stretched myself and wrote this journal too! The lesson here is when you commit to a goal, you will realize that your fears are not as big as you think. In fact, you will learn that you are more capable, more competent, and more qualified than you ever thought to realize your dreams. Joy is contagious. I got so inspired that I am now writing my third book. Remember, nothing has ever been accomplished without action. Half of your battle is starting with one simple action. This journal is meant to propel you to do just that…START!

My four keys to success were:

1. Write attainable goals that can be accomplished in one year.
2. Confess your fears so you can move past them.
3. Create your tribe of dream builders for support and accountability.
4. Share your goal with everyone. Speak it and affirm it out loud so you continue to commit to action. "The tongue has the power of life and death, and those who love it will eat its fruit." (Proverbs 18:21 NIV)

Dream Building Goals

What goals would you like to have accomplished this time next year?

Today's date:______________________________________

Goal #1:

____

____

Goal #2:

____

____

Goal #3:

____

____

Stretch Goal #4:

____

____

Stretch Goal #5:

____

____

Letter of Confession

One of the key areas that hold us back from goal attainment is FEAR. So, we need to acknowledge and remove fear from the equation of success. As mentioned previously, one of the ways in which I conquer my fears is by confessing them.

Write a private letter to yourself that you will read one year later. In the letter, share your fears, things that are holding you back, and feelings of unhappiness or disappointment. You should be as vulnerable as possible in writing all your feelings about where you are in your life right now. Share why you have not been successful in attaining your goals thus far.

Write the letter, date it, and seal it in an envelope. Place the letter in this journal. Every time you open this journal, the sealed envelope will serve as a reminder of your commitment to investing in your happiness. It will be a visible cue of where you were and where you want to go. It will signal that you are worth this journey and your future days will be better than your former days. It will show that you are willing to invest in YOU. One year from now, you will read the letter and be amazed by how far you have come. You will see progress, from the small to the mind-blowing, if you commit to *Journal to JOY*.

Now it's time to write the letter. After you have written it, you are ready to start the journey of deep thought and reflection. I believe in you and encourage you through this process as you will become the master of your joy and happiness.

Who Are Your Dream Builders?

Dream builders are the people in your life who have demonstrated success in the area(s) in which you want to accomplish your goals. They either have experience, knowledge, opportunity, or access to help you to achieve your goals. Avoid individuals who are negative or who have not accomplished the things in which you are trying to attain. Dream builders are role models, coaches, and mentors.

List your dream builders:
1.
2.
3.

Why are they a dream builder?

(What have they accomplished that can help you?)

____

____

____

____

____

____

____

____

SA Phillips, one of the contributors to ***The Journey to Joy***, has found great success through her S.T.A.N.D. principle which means to Stop Taking Advice from Non-Doers. Evaluate your relationships and determine with whom you may need to take a S.T.A.N.D.

Who are the people that you need to stop taking advice from?

____

____

____

____

____

____

____

____

____

WEEK 1
WHO ARE YOU?

"I knew you before I formed you in your mother's womb. Before you were born I set you apart and appointed you as my prophet to the nations."
– (Jeremiah 1:5 NLT)

Reflection questions:
- ❖ Who are you?
- ❖ What is your divine appointment in life?
- ❖ Name three words that describe your current life.
- ❖ What new beginnings and memories do you want to create?
- ❖ What bad habits do you want to end?

____

____

____

____

____

____

____

____

____

____

____

____

____

____

____

____

____

____

____

____

____

____

____

____

____

____

"You were created with purpose. Now own it and live." Joy

Affirmation: _______________________________

____

____

WEEK 2
WHAT IS YOUR FOUNDATION?

"A good name is more desirable than great riches;
to be esteemed is better than silver or gold."
— (Proverbs 22:1 NIV)

Reflection Questions:

❖ Think of a memory or experience that helped define your foundation. What is it? How did it develop you into who you are today?

❖ What does your name mean and how was it chosen?

❖ What do you love about your life? (Find something to be grateful for)

❖ One year from now, what do you want your life to look like? What goals would make you live a more joyful life?

____

____

____

____

____

____

____

____

____

____

____

____

____

____

____

____

____

____

____

____

____

____

"My name is my purpose." – Joy

Affirmation: ___________________________

____

____

WEEK 3
DOUBT

"Doubt kills more dreams that failure ever will."
— unknown

Reflection Questions:
- ❖ Think about a time in your life where you struggled with doubt.
- ❖ How do you conquer doubt?
- ❖ What role has faith played in your life?

____

____

____

____

____

____

____

____

____

____

____

____

____

____

"Faith says to go as far as you can see and when you get there, you will see farther. Faith is the key to remove doubt." – Taylor

Affirmation: ________________________________

____

____

WEEK 4
DO YOU HAVE A QUALITY RELATIONSHIP?

"It takes both sides to build a bridge."
– Fredrik Nael

Reflection Questions:
- ❖ What do you and your spouse or best friend do together, just with each other?
- ❖ How have you allowed children, work, or friendships to take the front stage of your relationship or friendship/marriage?
- ❖ What immediate actions can you take to invest more quality time in your relationship?

____

____

____

____

____

____

____

____

____

"Approach life changes as opportunities to grow in your marriage. It's okay to redefine US!"

– Ann

Affirmation: _______________________________

____

WEEK 5
PRAYER

"God speaks in the silence of the heart. Listening is the beginning of prayer." – Mother Teresa

Reflection Questions:

- ❖ What are your most urgent prayers?
- ❖ Describe a time in which you had to rely on faith.
- ❖ What is one miracle that you have witnessed?
- ❖ Describe an unanswered prayer where you still have faith.

____

____

____

____

____

____

____

____

____

____

____

____

____

____

____

____

____

"There is a God that answers prayers." – Joy

Affirmation: _______________________________

____

____

WEEK 6
REGRETS

"I regret nothing in my life, even if my past was full of hurt, I still look back and smile because it made me who I am today." – unknown

Reflection Questions:
- ❖ What is your most embarrassing moment and why?
- ❖ What do you regret giving up or stopping?
- ❖ What caused you to give up or stop? Would you do things differently if you had the opportunity?

____

____

____

____

____

____

____

____

____

"Never let embarrassment rule your life. It's just one moment in time." – Taylor

Affirmation: ________________________________

____

____

WEEK 7
TRUST YOUR GUT

"Intuition does not come to an unprepared mind."
– Einstein

Reflection Questions:
- ❖ Think about a time when you did something that didn't feel right. Why did you do it?
- ❖ How do you deal with uncertainty? Do you panic, remain calm, etc.?
- ❖ What lessons have "intuition" taught you?

____

____

____

____

____

____

____

____

____

____

____

"If it doesn't feel right, don't do it!" – Ann

Affirmation: _______________________________

____

____

WEEK 8
COPING WITH LOSS

"The fear of death follows from the fear of life. A man who lives is fully prepared to die at any time." – Mark Twain

Reflection Questions:
- ❖ What has been your greatest struggle in life?
- ❖ What has brought you the greatest joy and why?
- ❖ How have you dealt with death or a significant loss?

____

____

____

____

____

____

____

____

____

____

____

____

____

____

____

____

____

____

____

____

____

____

____

____

____

____

____

"My joy is my strength." – Charity

Affirmation: ______________________________

____

____

WEEK 9
RESPECT

"It doesn't matter what people call you; it matters what you answer to." – Ruth

Reflection Questions:

- ❖ Have you ever felt marginalized in life? When and why?
- ❖ How did you handle the situation? Did you stand up for yourself or did you relent and give up keeping the peace? If so, why or why not?
- ❖ Describe your "true" self if no one was watching?
- ❖ Why do you hide aspects of yourself?

____

____

____

____

____

____

____

____

____

____

____

____

____

____

____

____

____

____

____

____

____

____

____

____

____

____

"Everyone deserves respect!" – Tyron Fitzgerald

Affirmation: _______________________________

____

____

WEEK 10
DIVERSITY

"One day I will get to rewrite history at my table." – Taylor

Reflection Questions:
- ❖ Have you ever, personally, experienced or witnessed racism? How did you feel?
- ❖ What did you do? Why or why not?
- ❖ How did you deal with your feelings?
- ❖ What lessons did you learn about yourself? About others?

____

____

____

____

____

____

____

____

____

____

____

____

____

____

____

____

"Inclusion does not mean I agree, it means I respect." – Joy

Affirmation: _______________________________

____

____

WEEK 11
INCLUSION

"I never thought I would be invited to a white man's table." – Ruth

Reflection Questions:

- ❖ Describe a time in your life where you felt "different."
- ❖ Where do you feel most included? Most excluded? Why?
- ❖ Are there people in your family who see the world differently than you? How can you help to expand their worldview?

____

____

____

____

____

____

____

____

____

____

"Inclusion is an experience in which you are both invited and welcomed." – Joy

Affirmation: _______________________________

WEEK 12
I PRAY FOR THE WORLD

"To truly be inclusive, the world needs more love and understanding." – Joy

Reflection Questions:

- ❖ Have you ever experienced racism or bias? If so, how did it impact you?
- ❖ Do you pray for the world? If so, what was your prayer?
- ❖ What has suprised you most as it relates to diversity and inclusion in your country?

____

____

____

____

____

____

____

____

____

____

____

____

____

____

____

____

____

____

____

____

____

____

____

____

"Coming together is a beginning. Keeping together is progress. Working together is success."
— Henry Ford

Affirmation: __________________________________

____

____

ONE SMALL

POSITIVE

THOUGHT

IN THE MORNING
CAN MAKE A POSITIVE

DIFFERENCE

TO THE WAY YOU LIVE
TODAY

WEEK 13
SURVIVING LOSS

*"Remember the good times and keep thanks in
your heart; that's your peace." – Ruth*

Reflection Questions:
- ❖ What is the deepest hurt you have experienced?
- ❖ Why was it the deepest?
- ❖ How have you coped or dealt with hurt or grief (Avoidance, denial, confronting, counseling, etc.)? Why?

"For to me, to live is Christ, and to die is gain."
(Philippians 1:21 KJV)

Affirmation: _______________________________

WEEK 14
PARENTAL STATUS

"God's will is perfect, even when it is difficult for me to accept." – Joy

Reflection Questions:
- ❖ Do you desire children? Why or why not?
- ❖ What are your fears or dreams regarding your parental status?
- ❖ What decisions or choices have you made regarding parental status? If you have children, what role do they play in your life?
- ❖ Describe the perfect parent. What qualities do you desire?

____

____

____

____

____

____

____

____

____

____

____

____

____

____

____

____

____

____

____

____

"Miscarriages are not an indication that something is wrong. You just have angels in the sky." — Joy

Affirmation: ____________________________________

____

____

WEEK 15
OBEDIENCE

"It is better to obey than to experience great sacrifice." – Charity

Reflection Questions:
- ❖ What have you sacrificed for love? Why?
- ❖ What experience has impacted you the most in life and why?
- ❖ What lesson has obedience taught you (good or bad)?

____

____

____

____

____

____

____

____

____

____

____

____

____

____

____

____

____

____

____

____

____

____

"Children, obey your parents in the Lord: for this is right. Honour thy father and mother; which is the first commandment with promise; That it may be well with thee, and thou mayest live long on the earth." (Ephesians 6:1-3 KJV)

Affirmation: ____________________________

____

____

WEEK 16
LOSING SOMEONE YOU LOVE

"The heart knows what the mind sometimes resists." – Kristy Sullivan

Reflection Questions:
- ❖ What do you need to let go to live?
- ❖ What is that one area in your life that is still hard to deal with or revisit? Why?
- ❖ If you have ever lost someone, how do you honor special dates like their birthday? Do you wallow in pain or do you celebrate?
- ❖ What is your greatest fear? How does it manifest in your life?

____

____

____

____

____

____

____

____

____

____

____

____

____

____

____

____

*"Spend your time celebrating the life versus
mourning the death." – Joy*

Affirmation: _______________________________

____

____

WEEK 17
MARRIAGE

"If you look for trouble, you most likely will find it." – Ruth

Reflection Questions:

* ❖ What example(s) of a successful marriage do you have in your family? What makes it/them successful?
* ❖ If married, how do you define success? If not married, how would you?
* ❖ Are you fulfilled in your relationship? How do you know? Why or why not?
* ❖ Do you like your spouse/boyfriend or girlfriend? Why or why not?

____

____

____

____

____

____

____

____

____

____

____

____

____

____

____

____

____

____

____

____

____

____

____

____

"Marriage requires work and self-sacrifice." – Joy

Affirmation: _______________________________

____

____

WEEK 18
MINDSET?

"A positive mindset is like having a super human power." – Tyron Fitzgerald Jr.

Reflection Questions:
- ❖ Are you a glass half full or half empty type of person? Why or why not?
- ❖ What or who has shaped the way in which you think or approach things in life? How has this influenced you?
- ❖ What gives you mental energy? What takes it away?

____

____

____

____

____

____

____

____

____

____

*"Your mind is strong enough to heal your body in
ways that science never can!"*
— Tyron Fitzgerald, Jr.

Affirmation: ______________________________

____

____

WEEK 19
STICK OR STAY?

"Marriage reveals the whole person. The good, bad, and sometimes ugly." – Ann

Reflection Questions:

❖ What is your definition of marriage? What are the core elements of a successful marriage?

❖ If married, have you ever thought of leaving? If so, why? What made you leave or stay?

❖ What were the secrets that you brought into marriage or relationship? How have those secrets impacted your relationship? What has been your biggest test?

❖ What made you stick or stay?

____

____

____

____

____

____

____

____

____

"If there is such a thing as a good marriage, it is because it resembles friendship rather than love."
— *Michel de Montaigne*

Affirmation: ____

GIVE YOUR
BEST GIFTS
TO THE
WORLD ...
AND SMILE!

WEEK 20
A PROMISE TO KEEP

"Be careful what you promise." – Ann

Reflection Questions:

- ❖ How do you define a promise? What is the last promise that you made? Why?
- ❖ What promise have you made that you really didn't intend to keep?
- ❖ How do you decline a promise versus being gracious?

____

____

____

____

____

____

____

____

____

____

____

____

____

____

____

____

____

____

____

____

____

____

____

____

____

____

____

____

____

"Your word is bond. It is the greatest testament of your integrity." – Joy

Affirmation: _______________________________

____

____

WEEK 21
THE BALL IS IN YOUR COURT

"If you can't beat them, you might have more fun joining." – Ann

Reflection Questions:

- ❖ What are your weekend rituals and do they provide an opportunity for you to enjoy hobbies or pleasures?
- ❖ Are you a sports fan? If so, how did you fall in love with sports?
- ❖ What hobby does your spouse or friend have that you could benefit from joining?
- ❖ What might be the advantages of trying something that your spouse or friend enjoys?

____

____

____

____

____

____

____

____

____

____

____

____

____

____

____

____

____

____

____

____

____

____

____

"Life is an endless process of self-discovery."
– James Gardner

Affirmation: _________________________

____

____

WEEK 22
RELATIONSHIPS

"Avoid unfulfilling relationships as if they were the plague." – Taylor

Reflection Questions:

- ❖ Have you ever had an "unstuffed teddy bear" relationship? Why was it unstuffed?
- ❖ What are your non-negotiable relationship standards?
- ❖ What advice have you received that left you unstuffed?
- ❖ What relationship is missing in your life and why?

____

____

____

____

____

____

____

____

____

____

"Set your OWN standards for your relationship." – Joy

Affirmation: _______________________

WEEK 23
IT'S NOT PERSONAL

"An angry person can't think." – Ann

Reflection Questions:
- ❖ What are your "hot buttons" in business settings? Why?
- ❖ How do you deal with anger? What are the pros and cons of this method?
- ❖ How do others experience you when you are angry? How long do you stay angry and why?

____

____

____

____

____

____

____

____

____

____

____

____

____

____

____

____

____

____

____

____

____

____

____

____

____

____

____

____

"An angry person can't think, and a thinking person can't be angry." – *Melvin Phillips*

Affirmation: _______________________________

____

____

WEEK 24
MY LITTLE BECAME MUCH

"Take whatever you have been given in life and make MUCH… that is the true definition of wealth." – Ruth

Reflection Questions:

- ❖ What does success look like in your life?
- ❖ How do you define family?
- ❖ What is your greatest treasure and why?
- ❖ Have you ever thought, my life would be so much better if I had more _________ (money, clothes, friends, etc.)? If so, how are you making wealth with what you already have?

____

____

____

____

____

____

____

____

____

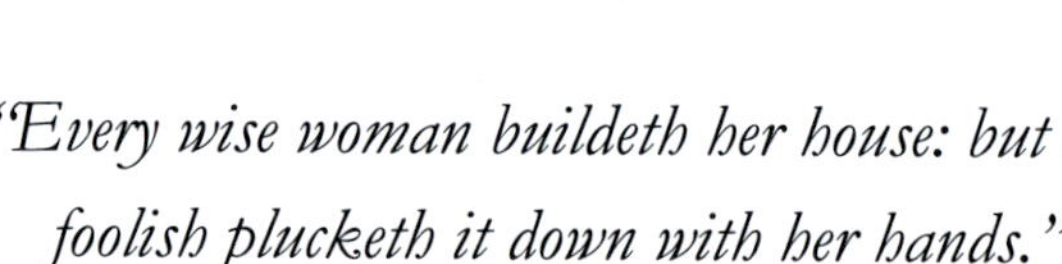

*"Every wise woman buildeth her house: but the
foolish plucketh it down with her hands."*
(Proverbs 14.1 KJV)

Affirmation: _______________________________

____

____

WEEK 25
CHANGE

"Growth comes from discomfort." – Taylor

Reflection Questions:

- ❖ What is the most significant change or challenge you've faced in life?
- ❖ How do you deal with change?
- ❖ What change do you regret? Why?

"Change is the necessary ingredient for growth."
— Melvin Phillips

Affirmation: ___________________________

WEEK 26
LESSONS FROM A FATHER

"Don't let anything rule you, you rule it. You should always stay in control of the situation."
– Charity

Reflection Questions:

❖ What do you remember about your childhood as it pertains to your father? How have those memories influenced you?

❖ What is a favorite memory of your father or mother?

❖ Have you ever had to take a herb or concoction as a child to get well? If so, what was it and why?

____

____

____

____

____

____

____

____

____

____

____

____

____

____

____

____

____

____

____

____

____

____

"A father teaches a girl how to be respected by a man." – Charity

Affirmation: _______________________________

____

____

WEEK 27
SELF-DISCOVERY

*"Every woman deserves "me" time. It's needed,
necessary, and fundamental to your happiness."*
— Joy

Reflection Questions:
- ❖ If you have ever felt lost, how did you go about finding yourself?
- ❖ If you currently feel lost, what is contributing to this feeling? What do you need to start, stop, or continue to help provide greater clarity and self-worth in your life?
- ❖ Are you happy? Why or why not?

____

____

____

____

____

____

____

____

____

____

____

____

____

"As women, we give up so much of ourselves that we sometimes forget to give TO OURSELVES." – Ann

Affirmation: _______________________________

____

____

WEEK 28
FRIENDSHIPS

"A friend is a reflection of who you are when no one is watching." – Tyron Fitzgerald, Jr

Reflection Questions:
- ❖ Who are your close friends and why?
- ❖ If you were a reflection of them, describe the picture or the visual that the world would see of you? (Values, beliefs, etc.)
- ❖ Would you be happy with what you saw in the mirror? Does it adequately describe who you think YOU are?

____

____

____

____

____

____

____

____

____

____

____
____
____
____
____
____
____
____
____
____
____
____
____
____
____

"Choose friends that help create the vision and the pathway to where you aspire to go in life."
— Tyron Fitzgerald

Affirmation: _______________________________

____
____

WEEK 29
I AM NOT A SUPERHERO

*"Wonder Woman is not real so don't be afraid to
ask for help!" – Ann*

Reflection Questions:

❖ What demands have you placed on yourself that seem overwhelming? Have you ever stopped and asked for help? Why or why not?

❖ What are the things in life that give you energy? What sucks or diminishes your energy? Why?

❖ What requirements or definitions of success were part of your upbringing that have shaped who you are today? Do you need to reject any of those teachings? If so, which one(s) and why?

"Why don't you ask him to help you?" – Ann

Affirmation: _______________________________

____

WEEK 30
VULNERABILITY WITH CHILDREN

"Your children should be comfortable with you when it matters most." – Taylor

Reflection Questions:

- ❖ Did you share any personal stories with your parents? Why or why not?
- ❖ If you have children, what level of comfort or safety have you provided for them to talk to you about private matters?
- ❖ How can you ensure that you are a trusted source and that you don't make people feel judged?
- ❖ Describe your true self.

"An open-door relationship with your parents is priceless!" – Taylor

Affirmation: _______________________________

____

____

WEEK 31
OUT OF THE BOX

"You don't have to fit in a box." – Taylor

Reflection Questions:

❖ In what activities do you engage on a regular basis to learn and grow?

❖ Have you ever considered yourself a dabbler? If so, why?

❖ Are you in a box, out of the box, or trying to find a box? Describe how you see yourself in the world.

____

____

____

____

____

____

____

____

____

____

____

____

____

____

____

____

____

____

____

____

____

____

____

____

____

"I have found joy out of the box." – *Taylor*

Affirmation: _______________________________

____

____

WEEK 32
WINNING

"Winning in life is an individual sport." – Joy

Reflection Questions:
- ❖ In which areas of your life are you fiercely and intentionally driven to win?
- ❖ How are you competing? Who are you competing against?
- ❖ How do you know if you are winning?

"You miss 100% of the shots that you don't take." – Wayne Gretzky

Affirmation: ___________________________

____

____

WEEK 33
WHAT IS YOUR PASSION?

"Never feel guilty for doing what you love."
– Ann

Reflection Questions:

- ❖ Have you ever felt guilty for doing something you love? Why or why not?
- ❖ Which childhood activity shaped your life? Why?
- ❖ With what experience have you had a love/hate relationship?

____

____

____

____

____

____

____

____

____

____

____

____

____

____

____

____

____

____

____

____

____

____

____

____

____

____

"Your passion is waiting for your courage to catch up!" – Isabelle Lafleche

Affirmation: _______________________________

____

____

WEEK 34
SELF IMAGE

"Look in the mirror, if you don't like what you see, make the changes needed." – Joy

Reflection Questions:

- ❖ Do you struggle with your weight? What excuses are you making (baby weight, middle-age spread, menopause, too many hours at work, etc.)?
- ❖ What are you indulging in that creates a short-term pleasure only to be a disappointment or regret later?
- ❖ Which new habits do you need to create to live a healthier life?

____

____

____

____

____

____

____

____

____

____

____

____

____

____

____

____

____

____

____

____

____

____

"You are beautiful just the way you are!" – Ann

Affirmation: _________________________

____

____

WEEK 35
PILLAR OF STRENGTH

"My joy is my strength." – Charity

Reflection Questions:
- ❖ Who is the pillar of strength in your family?
- ❖ Describe a time in your life in which you had to rely on a higher level of strength? What were the things or people that gave you hope?
- ❖ What is the legacy you want to leave and why?

"Now also when I am old and gray-headed, O God, forsake me not; until I have shewed thy strength unto this generation, and thy power to everyone this is to come."(Psalm 71:18 KJV)

Affirmation: _______________________________

____

____

WEEK 36
FEAR

"When you are afraid, you will find peace in prayer. God answers prayers." – Charity

Reflection Questions:

❖ In what situation have you had to face fear?

❖ What is your greatest fear and why?

❖ Share a story in which you conquered fear.

❖ What is one thing you can do differently when faced with fear?

"Courage is resistance to fear, mastery of fear, not absence of fear." – Mark Twain

Affirmation: ______________________________

WEEK 37
HEALTH

"Know your body, examine your body, and listen to your body." – Taylor

Reflection Questions:

- ❖ How would you describe your health and why?
- ❖ What fears do you have regarding your health?
- ❖ How often do you pray and how does it impact your mental health?

____

____

____

____

____

____

____

____

____

____

____

____

____

"Your largest fear carries your greatest growth."
— unknown

Affirmation: _______________________________

____

____

WEEK 38
SUPPORTING WOMEN

"Every woman needs a good girdle. It teaches your body how to stay tight." – Joy

Reflection Questions:
- ❖ Which friend could you offer more love and support? Why?
- ❖ What have you experienced in your body that you struggle with but refuse to acknowledge?
- ❖ How can you better support the internal healing that women need as they experience different stages of life?

"Choose what is right for you and your body."
– *Ann*

Affirmation: _______________________________

WEEK 39
EDUCATION

"Education is the most powerful weapon you can use to change the world." – Nelson Mandela

Reflection Questions:

- ❖ On a daily basis, how do you seek new information and learning?
- ❖ What educational goals do you have? Have you attained them? If not, what is in your way?
- ❖ What immediate actions can you take in your educational journey?
- ❖ Write about a time in which you were challenged in an academic setting? How did it grow you?

____

____

____

____

____

____

____

____

____

____

____

____

____

____

____

____

"Children must be taught how to think, not what to think." – Margaret Mead

Affirmation: _______________________________

____

____

WEEK 40
SAYING GOODBYE

"Not every friend will be a lifelong friend and that is not a bad thing." - Taylor

Reflection Questions:

- ❖ What are the friendships or relationships in your life that bring you great joy? Why?
- ❖ Identify the friendships/relationships that cause you pain or unhappiness? Why do you stay in these relationships?
- ❖ What actions do you need to take to remove people and relationships that no longer add to your happiness?

____

____

____

____

____

____

____

____

____

____

____

____

____

____

____

____

____

____

____

____

____

____

____

____

"A true friend is someone who gives you total freedom to be yourself." — unknown

Affirmation: _______________________

____

____

2 signs that show you are living your purpose:

1. People experience growth and purpose in what you are doing.

2. Haters try to block and stop your progress.

WEEK 41
LIVING YOUR BEST LIFE

"The decisions that you make will have a lasting impact on you. That is why it is vital to make decisions that will make you happy in the long run." – Taylor

Reflection Questions:

* What decision have you made that you regret? Why?
* Who do you desire to make happy other than yourself? Why?
* Think about a time in which you made a big decision. Whose advice did you take? Why? Would you do things differently if you had the chance?

____

____

____

____

____

____

____

"Don't let life happen to you. Make life happen."
— Taylor

Affirmation: _________________________________

____

____

WEEK 42
MARRY YOUR BEST FRIEND

"Marriage is one of the best decisions I've ever made." – Joy

Reflection Questions:
- ❖ How do you define the perfect marriage?
- ❖ If married, is your spouse your best friend? Why or why not?
- ❖ What would a best friend relationship look like for you? Please be specific.
- ❖ Would you marry the same person again? Why or why not? If not married, describe your non-negotiables for marriage.

____

____

____

____

____

____

____

____

____

____

"A long, successful marriage exists because you
<u>like</u> the person, not just love them." — Joy

Affirmation: _______________________________

WEEK 43
SACRIFICE IN RELATIONSHIPS

"No sacrifice is without great reward."
— unknown

Reflection Questions:

❖ What sacrifice(s) have you made for marriage or a relationship? Was it worth it? Why or why not?

❖ What do you do differently or give up to make others happy?

❖ How has your relationship or friendship grown you or made you better?

____

____

____

____

____

____

____

____

____

____

____

____

____

____

____

____

____

____

____

____

____

____

____

____

"I learned to trust my husband and believe in him even when the path is not clear to me." – Joy

Affirmation: ___________________________

____

____

WEEK 44
CREATE YOUR OWN RULES

*"Just know, we don't have to repeat everything
our parents did." – Joy*

Reflection Questions:

❖ What norms or cultural values are different in your home than how you were raised? Why or why not?

❖ Are there areas in your life in which you are waiting for permission or acceptance from your family? If so, what are those areas and why?

❖ What is the help that you need that you haven't asked for? What is preventing you from asking? What immediate steps can you take to get help?

____

____

____

____

____

____

____

____

____

*"Keep the good and replace the old with new more
efficient habits." – Joy*

Affirmation: ___________________________________

____

____

WEEK 45
CHILDREN

"My children are my greatest joy and I've enjoyed raising them." – Joy

Reflection Questions:

❖ What are your dreams or hopes for your children or for the children in your family?

❖ How do you ensure that they experience gentleness? Love? Respect? Being heard?

❖ What steps do you need to take to be more present in your child(ren)'s life? Or the children you love?

❖ What is the greatest lesson you want them to remember in life?

____

____

____

____

____

____

____

____

____

____

____

____

____

____

____

____

____

____

____

____

____

____

____

____

"Our children are a reflection of what we have done right or done wrong!" – unknown

Affirmation: _______________________________

____

____

WEEK 46
STRESS

"Do not conform to the pattern of this world, but be transformed by the renewing of your mind. Then you will be able to test and approve what God's will is—his good, pleasing and perfect will." – (Romans 12:2 NIV)

Reflection Questions:

- What is causing stress in your life and why?
- How does worry show up in your life? What does it impact (mood, sleep, eating habits, health, relationships, etc.)?
- How do you know when you are stressed?
- What habits do you need to begin to reduce stress in your life?

____

____

____

____

____

____

____

____

"The greatest weapon over stress is our ability to choose one thought over another."
— William James

Affirmation: ___________________________

____

WEEK 47
DON'T GIVE UP

"Patience is a delightful and precious virtue."
— Unknown

Reflection Questions:
- ❖ What is an area in life that exhausts your or takes away your energy?
- ❖ Describe your current feelings for an unanswered prayer or life wish/dream.
- ❖ How do you encourage or inspire yourself? Do you wait for others to affirm or build you up? What does that look like in your life?

____

____

____

____

____

____

____

____

____

____

____

____

____

____

____

"Patience is also a form of action."
— Auguste Rodin

Affirmation: _______________________________

____

____

WEEK 48
DON'T FORGET

"You are a source of strength, if only you knew it." — Joy

Reflection Questions:

- ❖ What are the things in your life that you have conquered and overcame?
- ❖ Detail one testimony in your life that serves as a great reminder of your strength?
- ❖ What is your greatest strength or best talent? Why? How are you using it to help the world?

____

____

____

____

____

____

____

____

____

____

____

____

____

____

____

____

____

____

____

____

____

____

____

____

____

____

____

"The joy of the lord is your strength."
— (Nehemiah 8:10 KJV)

Affirmation: ________________________________

____

____

WEEK 49
HUMILITY

"The humility and fear of the Lord lead to riches, honor and long life." – (Proverbs 22:4)

Reflection Questions:
- ❖ How do you define humility?
- ❖ Would your family/friends describe you as humble? Why or why not?
- ❖ How could you be more intentional in demonstrating humility? How might this improve your life?

____

____

____

____

____

____

____

____

____

____

____

____

____

____

____

____

____

____

____

____

____

____

____

____

____

"Humility is one of the best traits of a leader."

— Joy

Affirmation: _______________________

____

____

WEEK 50
RESOLUTION

"Why God?" – Unknown

Reflection Questions:
- ❖ What are the question marks in your life right now?
- ❖ What are the things that you struggle to understand and resolve? How are you dealing with this?
- ❖ What are the steps you need to take to resolve and let go of the unanswered questions in your life?

____

____

____

____

____

____

____

____

____

____

"Now our knowledge is partial and incomplete, and even the gift of prophecy reveals only part of the whole picture." – (1 Corinthians 13:9 NLT)

Affirmation: _______________________________

WEEK 51
NO BAD DAYS

"I have good days and better days, because I do not have bad days." – Ann

Reflection Questions:

- ❖ Do you ever refer to your day as "bad"? Why or why not?
- ❖ What constitutes a "good" day or a "bad" day for you? How do approach them differently?
- ❖ What could you do differently to have "good" days?

____

____

____

____

____

____

____

____

____

____

____

____

____

____

____

"This is the day that the lord has made, we will rejoice and be glad in it." (Psalm 18:24)

Affirmation: _______________________________

____

____

YOU ARE THE AUTHOR OF YOUR STORY.

DO NOT LET ANYONE ELSE AUTHOR YOUR STORY.

OWN IT AND TELL IT RIGHT!

WEEK 52
FORGIVENESS

"The world needs more love and forgiveness. You can't have love without forgiveness." – Joy

Reflection Questions:

- ❖ What do you need to forgive yourself for? Has it been difficult to do? Why?
- ❖ Describe a hurt, pain, or experience that is hard for you to let go or forgive? Why does it still affect you?
- ❖ How do you show or demonstrate forgiveness? How do others KNOW and experience it from you?

____

____

____

____

____

____

____

____

____

"Forgiveness is more than a word. It is a state of loving a person more than they hurt you." – Joy

Affirmation: ___________________________

____

____

EPILOGUE

Lastly, I share one of the stories from the *Journey to Joy*. The story is called *Kingdom Fruit*. This is a story of my 100-year-old great grandmother's prayer for our family. I hope you enjoy it.

KINGDOM FRUIT

*"I want to be able to bring forth fruit fit for
God's kingdom." – Charity*

One day, when pregnant with my first child, I was at my father's house. One of his sisters was visiting as well. She was a widow and a missionary in the church. She wanted children and unfortunately, couldn't have any. She was talking to my father about Hannah. She had read about Hannah in the Bible and she was sharing the story about Hannah talking to the Lord about having a child. Hannah had tried for so long and had not been able to conceive. She asked the Lord to bless her where she would be able to bring forth a son. If he did, she would give him back to the Lord.

There I was, pregnant and sitting in the next room, listening to their conversation. I had been praying for months that I wouldn't die when I had the baby. My mother died in childbirth so that fear was real for me. After my aunt went home, the Lord gave me these words:

"Lord strengthen and able me to bring forth fruit fit for your kingdom. Bless me to have a missionary; let me be a missionary. If you give me this, I will give the baby back to you."

I didn't tell anyone about my prayer. I didn't only pray the prayer during that pregnancy, I prayed it every time I was pregnant. I tried to live what I prayed. God heard me and answered my prayers. I was blessed with eight beautiful and healthy children, four boys and four girls (Jorene, Ruth, Perry, LC, James, Lois, Willie, and Berlinda).

I taught them to respect me and to obey. I also taught them to laugh and play, to have fun. As long as we were together, we were happy. I was blessed and honored to have fruit from my family tree, my eight gifts from God. I meant those words that I prayed on that day. I gave each one of them back to God and God answered my prayer. I had two missionaries, one pastor, one assistant pastor, two deacons, and six choir members within my eight children.

All of them are faithful to God, the church, and their families. They are my KINGDOM FRUIT. I now pray for every generation to come. I have five generations of fruit living in my family to continue my prayer for the kingdom.

"Now also when I am old and gray-headed, O God, forsake me not; until I have shewed thy strength unto this generation, and thy power to everyone that is to come." Psalm 71:18 KJV

I HOPE YOU HAVE FOUND MORE SELF
DISCOVERY AND HAPPINESS THROUGH
THIS JOURNAL!

For speaking engagement requests, please email
joyfitzgerald@speakingjoy.org

Interact with other *Journey to Joy* and *Journal to Joy* readers by joining the online community!

@SpeakingJoy